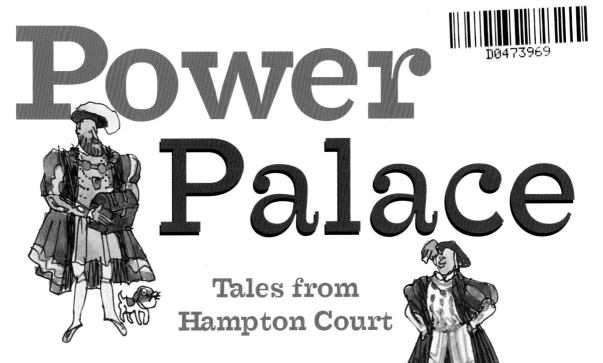

Power Palace

Tales from Hampton Court

Contents

Welcome...

...to Hampton Court Palace! It's almost **500** years old and ENORMOUS. There are over **1,000** rooms spread over 6 acres. You could fit 6 football pitches in it!

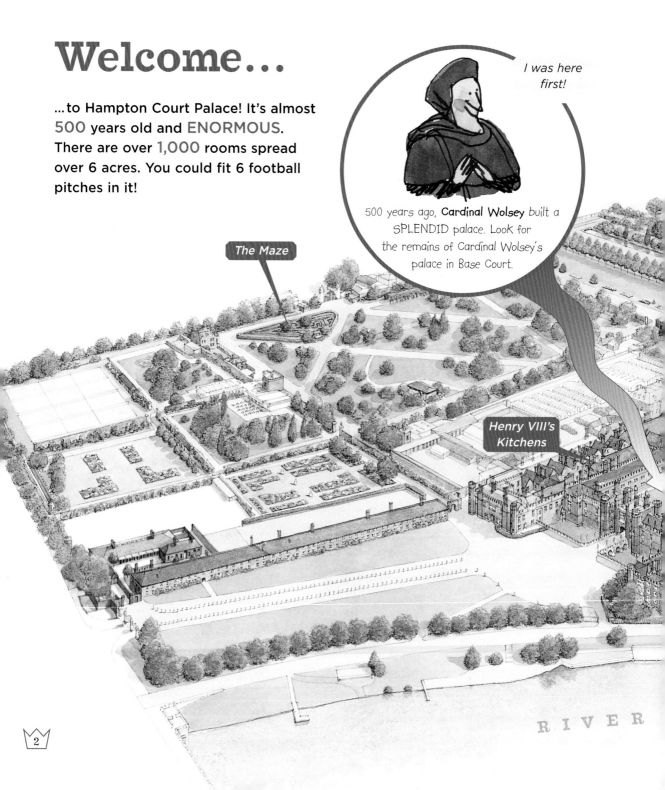

I was here first!

500 years ago, **Cardinal Wolsey** built a SPLENDID palace. Look for the remains of Cardinal Wolsey's palace in Base Court.

The Maze

Henry VIII's Kitchens

R I V E R

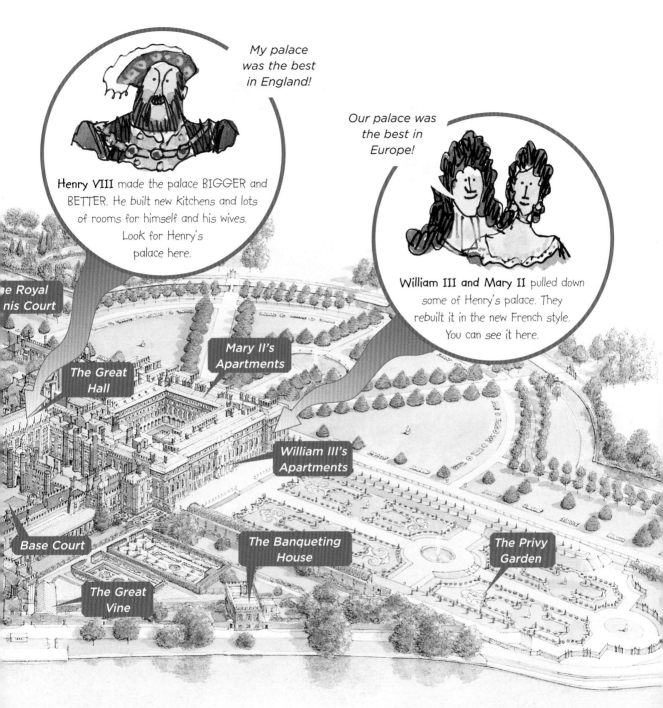

My palace was the best in England!

Henry VIII made the palace BIGGER and BETTER. He built new kitchens and lots of rooms for himself and his wives. Look for Henry's palace here.

Our palace was the best in Europe!

William III and Mary II pulled down some of Henry's palace. They rebuilt it in the new French style. You can see it here.

e Royal nis Court

Mary II's Apartments

The Great Hall

William III's Apartments

Base Court

The Banqueting House

The Privy Garden

The Great Vine

THAMES

Magnificent palaces

Hampton Court Palace is one of the most famous buildings in Britain. One queen was married and two princes and a princess were born here. Two queens died in the palace. Another is said to haunt it!

Palaces were built to show how clever, powerful and rich their owners were. They were stuffed with the finest paintings, tapestries and furniture. Wonderful music and plays were performed there and people wore the latest fashions. **Wow!**

▼ *Kings and queens welcomed important foreign visitors in their palaces. Here, Elizabeth I meets Dutch messengers.*

▼ *Hampton Court is about 15 miles from central London. 500 years ago the journey took half a day by river and one day by road.*

LOOK OUT FOR...

...the King's Beasts. The signs and badges they carry showed visitors that Henry came from a long line of kings.

Plenty of palaces

Kings and queens had lots of grand houses and palaces, mostly near London. Henry VIII had about 60! The largest and most important was the Palace of Whitehall, which was used for government. The Tower of London sheltered kings and queens in times of unrest. Hampton Court, which was in the country then, was a summer palace. The air was cleaner here, so kings and queens came to Hampton Court to escape the dreaded plague and other illnesses.

▲ At Hampton Court, kings and queens loved to go hunting in the parks.

The royal court

The royal family moved from palace to palace taking the court with them (advisers, nobles and servants). Sometimes they spent only hours there, sometimes a few months.

Palaces were great places for wonderful parties.

Well done

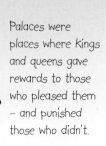

Palaces were places where kings and queens gave rewards to those who pleased them – and punished those who didn't.

All those people

All sorts of people surrounded the king and queen. Between them, they did everything from cleaning floors to wiping the king's bottom.

The most powerful people at court were ministers and churchmen who helped to govern the country. There were also rich noblemen hoping to introduce their sons to important people. Artists, musicians, entertainers, doctors and craftsmen provided the best of everything. Lastly, there were hundreds of servants scurrying around.

▲ This official in the court of Henry VIII wears royal initials. Can you spot 'H' for Henry?

◀ Henry VIII's velvet-covered toilet probably looked a bit like this one made for William III.

No entry!

The rooms at Hampton Court were arranged in strict order – and there were firm rules about where people could and couldn't go. Only very important people went through the Great Hall to the State Apartments where they MIGHT be allowed to see the king.

Only royalty were allowed to wear purple or gold.

◀ The Great Hall was the largest room in the palace. Most people met and ate here.

POOH!

The Groom of the Stool wiped the king's bottom with a cloth and got rid of any horrid smells!

Less important people at court shared the same toilet. It could seat 28 men!

◀ Check out these carved heads, high up on the roof of the Great Hall? Imagine what gossip they overheard!

Room for a little one

Lavish luxury

Cardinal Wolsey was Henry VIII's chief minister. He made Hampton Court into a luxurious palace. Then Henry seized it and made it larger and even more splendid.

Cardinal Wolsey fell out with Henry when the King wanted a divorce from his first wife, Katherine of Aragon. Henry took Hampton Court and gave Wolsey just four days to get out. What a **panic!**

▲ *After Henry, Cardinal Wolsey was the most powerful man in the country.*

Henry was very **rich** and **powerful**. He could afford the best. He set about making Hampton Court a magnificent palace to impress people – making sure they knew a great king lived here.

▲ *The Tudor Rose, the badge of Henry VIII and other Tudor kings and queens.*

◄ *Henry remodelled the Chapel Royal.*

LOOK OUT FOR...

...the tapestries. They were made with real gold and silver thread and could cost as much as a fully manned warship.

Inside and out

Henry doubled the size of Wolsey's palace. He had the inside decorated with brightly coloured woodwork and lots and lots of gold. Outside Henry built tiltyards for jousts (mock fights on horseback), archery butts, bowling alleys and tennis courts.

The palace had all the latest mod cons too. Fresh water was piped to the palace from Coombe Hill in Kingston, about three miles away.

When Hampton Court was finished in 1540, it was the most luxurious and up-to-date palace in the country.

Nicholas Oursian made ▷ this Astronomical Clock in 1541. It shows the time, month, day, the signs of the zodiac and even low and high tide at London Bridge.

Shoo! shoo! go away

The huge Cardinal spider is only found around Hampton Court. Legend says it lives in the shadow of Cardinal Wolsey. So watch out!

Henry even had hot running water in his bathroom.

Henry VIII and his wives

Henry had **SIX** wives. All of them visited Hampton Court and most had rooms specially built for them here.

Henry was married to his first wife, **Katherine of Aragon** for over 20 years. Henry and Katherine had a daughter (later Mary I) but Henry was desperate for a son to succeed him. When Katherine became too old to have children, Henry divorced her.

▲ *Katherine of Aragon, Henry's first wife.*

Henry's second wife was **Anne Boleyn**. She had a daughter (later Elizabeth I) but there was still no son. Henry **had** to get rid of her. Poor Anne was wrongly accused of being unfaithful and was beheaded at the Tower of London.

◄ *Henry was about 40 years old when this portrait was painted.*

Anne Boleyn chose to be beheaded with a sword rather than the usual axe.

▲ This is Anne Boleyn's badge.

Two weeks later, Henry married his third and favourite wife, Jane Seymour. She gave birth to Edward (later Edward VI) at Hampton Court, but sadly Jane died here soon afterwards.

Henry was delighted when he saw a portrait of Anne of Cleves, his fourth wife-to-be. Unfortunately, when Anne arrived Henry decided she wasn't pretty enough. He divorced her as quickly as possible!

Days later, Henry married his fifth wife, Catherine Howard. It is said that Henry was in the Chapel Royal praying when someone told him that Catherine, who was just a teenager, had a young boyfriend. Furious, he had her arrested. She dodged her guards and ran to the Chapel to plead for her life, but Henry locked her out. She, too, was beheaded at the Tower of London.

▲ Catherine Howard

Henry married Kateryn Parr, his sixth wife, in the Queen's Closet next to the Chapel Royal. By now he was old, sick and very fat. Henry died four years later in 1547.

COME BACK HENRY!

HENRY!

Henry thought Anne of Cleves looked like a horse!

The ghost of Catherine Howard is said to visit the Haunted Gallery.

Edward, Mary and Elizabeth

Henry's three children all stayed at Hampton Court.

Happy times

When Henry died his son Edward, aged 9, became king. Edward was too young to rule so his uncle, the Duke of Somerset, stepped in. Edward loved Hampton Court. He went for walks in the gardens, hunted in the parks, went shooting and played games on horseback.

▲ Prince Edward's christening took place in the Chapel Royal at Hampton Court. Can you spot the baby being carried in the procession? Princess Mary follows behind.

▲ This is Henry with Jane Seymour and their son Prince Edward. On the left is Princess Mary and on the right, Princess Elizabeth. The scene wasn't real. Can you work out why? Answer on page 35.

Sad times

In 1553, Edward died aged 15 and his half-sister Mary became queen. She married Philip II of Spain and soon announced she was expecting a baby. Mary came to Hampton Court for the birth but months later it became clear that the Queen wasn't having a baby after all. Sadly, stomach cancer had caused Mary's swollen tummy and she died in 1558.

Good times

On the day Mary died, Elizabeth became queen. During her reign she often visited Hampton Court. She watched tilts, plays and masques (plays with dance and music) here. She entertained friends including Sir Walter Ralegh, important guests and even a king who hoped to marry her.

▲ Queen Elizabeth I in her coronation robes.

Elizabeth built this ▷ fountain at Hampton Court. It squirted water at visitors when they weren't expecting it!

Hilarious your majesty

Elizabeth caught smallpox while staying at Hampton Court but she recovered.

Barnaby FitzPatrick shared lessons with Edward. But if Edward misbehaved, Barnaby got punished!

13

Fabulous feasts

▼ Everybody's food except the king's or queen's was cooked in the Great Kitchen. Their meals were cooked in their private kitchens.

Food facts

People ate lots of meat in Tudor times. In one year, the court ate:

- *8,200 sheep*
- *2,330 deer*
- *1,870 pigs*
- *1,240 oxen*
- *760 calves*
- *53 wild boar*

When kings and queens and the court stayed at the palace, everyone had to be fed. That meant two meals a day for at least 800 people in summer and even more in winter. Phew!

Meat and poultry came from hunts, farmers and markets. The palace reared its own rabbits and pheasants. Meat wasn't eaten on Fridays, some Wednesdays and during Lent for religious reasons, so people ate lots of fish too.

On feast days people ate swans and peacocks.

Eating in shifts

Most people ate in the Great Hall. But there were so many of them they had to eat in two shifts! More important people ate next door in the Great Watching Chamber. Henry ate by himself in his own dining room while his nobles stood and watched.

▲ *Bakers take bread from the oven.*

Henry VIII's favourite Jellied Milk

Make this jellied milk – a favourite dish at Tudor feasts. Ask a grown-up to help you before you start.

You will need:
- a packet of jelly
- 1/2 cup of hot water • 1pt milk
- a jelly mould

To make:

1 Cut the jelly into squares and put in a basin.

2 Pour on the hot water and stir until the jelly has melted.

3 Add the milk to the jelly and stir together.

4 Pour into the mould and leave to set.

5 Turn out on to a plate. Delicious!

LOOK OUT FOR...

...the wine cellars. Servants drank ale, a sort of watery beer. Important people drank wine – and lots of it!

more wine!

For great feasts marzipan was made into the shape of churches, castles and animals.

All change

Elizabeth I, the last Tudor monarch, died in 1603. She had no children so the throne passed to the Stuart kings of Scotland.

The first Stuart king, James I was clever. When he visited Hampton Court he invited other brainy people here to talk about the important topics of the day. In 1604 James held a great religious meeting at the palace when it was decided to translate the Bible from Greek and Hebrew into English.

▲ *James VI of Scotland and I of England.*

A doomed king

Charles I became king in 1625. Later he quarrelled with Parliament and Civil War broke out. The Parliamentarians, led by Oliver Cromwell, seized Hampton Court. After losing several battles Charles was imprisoned here in 1647.

▲ *Charles I and Queen Henrietta Maria befriended a dwarf called Jeffrey Hudson. He was only 46cm tall when he was 8. Can you see him in this picture?*

Down with the king!

As a prisoner Charles was treated well and was allowed visits from his friends and family. So imagine how cross Cromwell was when he learnt that Charles had escaped. Two years later Charles was recaptured and beheaded outside the Palace of Whitehall.

For the next nine years, Oliver Cromwell governed Britain. Under his rule many of the paintings and other treasures at Hampton Court were sold off or destroyed. But Cromwell kept the art he liked!

▲ Unlike kings, Oliver Cromwell had his portrait painted as he really was – including big warts!

Cromwell brought this statue ▷ to Hampton Court. Today, you can see it in Bushy Park.

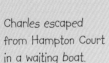

Charles escaped from Hampton Court in a waiting boat.

Cromwell liked to drink and eat with his soldiers. But, when he stayed at Hampton Court he slept in the queen's bed!

Long live the king!

In 1660, Charles II became king. He was really excited about his new palace and bought LOTS of new furniture and other gorgeous things for it.

People were overjoyed to have a king back on the throne. And Charles made the most of the happy atmosphere and held wonderful parties at Hampton Court.

◀ *Charles II was tall, handsome and witty.*

▼ *Charles II and his bride arrive at Hampton Court for their honeymoon. Look how many people they are bringing with them!*

from Portsmouth to Hampton court.

o Rainha Dona Catarina de Portsmuit ver a Hampton-court

Charles married Catherine of Braganza, a Portuguese princess and they spent their honeymoon at Hampton Court. Catherine was given a splendid new green velvet four-poster bed topped with feathery plumes.

Lovely

Charles II's girlfriends

Charles loved girls - and they loved him! Although he was married to Catherine he had lots of girlfriends. One of his favourites was Barbara Villiers. He even made her a Lady of the Queen's Bedchamber. Poor Catherine must have been very upset.

▲ Barbara Villiers lived at Hampton Court with her children by Charles II.

▲ Charles loved playing tennis and had the tennis courts rebuilt.

In 1666 Charles sent some of his possessions to Hampton Court by river to keep them safe from the Great Fire of London.

Lovely

Anne Hyde, Charles's sister-in-law, suggested that he had portraits painted of the best looking women in his court – including her!

HAVE YOU SEEN THE CAT?

Spend, spend, spend!

⚠ *Sir Christopher Wren designed the new palace in the latest French style.*

William III and Mary II became king and queen in 1689. William suffered from asthma. He chose Hampton Court as his main palace because the air was cleaner here.

William and Mary asked Sir Christopher Wren to give Hampton Court a **huge** makeover. They wanted something grander than the French king's luxurious palace at Versailles. And they wanted it **now!** Sir Christopher Wren, the architect, decided to pull everything down except the Great Hall. Luckily time and money ran out and only the King's and Queen's main rooms were rebuilt.

Hundreds of builders, brick-makers, masons, sculptors, carpenters and painters worked round the clock. The building went up so quickly that some of it fell down, killing two workmen.

LOOK OUT FOR...

...William's and Mary's initials linked together. You can find them inside carved in wood and outside carved in stone.

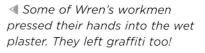
◄ *Some of Wren's workmen pressed their hands into the wet plaster. They left graffiti too!*

Mary was in charge of the rebuilding while William was away fighting.

▲ *The King's Staircase was the grand entrance to William III's Apartments. As you climb the stairs look out for William's hero, the Greek god Hercules, with his lion skin and club.*

The dreaded pox

Half way through the building works Mary died of smallpox and work stopped. Four years later, Whitehall Palace burnt down so William decided to carry on with the rebuilding of Hampton Court.

Hurrah for Mr. Nice

William loved drinking chocolate. He had a special cook called Mr Nice who made it for him.

William was scared of his enemies. He had special locks fitted on his bedroom door so he could lock himself in at night.

A glimpse of the king

The rooms in William's new palace were planned and decorated with special rules in mind.

In William's day, kings and queens were still the most powerful people in the country. To prevent royalty being pestered for favours, rules were made so that only certain people were allowed to speak to them.

Most of the court was allowed to go into the outer rooms. But only the King and the Groom of the Stool were allowed into the inner rooms. In between were rooms for special ceremonies – but only the King was allowed to sit down!

▲ *The Great Bedchamber was where the king was dressed each morning in front of his most important nobles and visitors.*

William's guards ▶ carried these spears decorated with his badge.

Important visitors watched the King get dressed, but they were kept back behind a rail.

Look at his fine coat

What a fine wig

What fine big underpants

Spare no expense!

The outer rooms were quite plain. But no expense was spared on the inner rooms. Walls were covered with silk and trimmed with gold and silver braid. Expensive tapestries and paintings were hung on top and there were magnificent carvings by Grinling Gibbons, the King's favourite craftsman.

William held ▶ ceremonies and received visitors in the Privy Chamber.

This is my room

No! I saw it first

The King and Queen had their own sets of rooms.

When the throne was empty people still had to bow to it.

Great gardens

William and Mary loved flowers and gardens. While Hampton Court was being updated, they had the gardens redesigned too.

William had spent many years planning gardens in his native country, Holland. Mary was very interested in gardening too. She had a famous collection of plants from all over the world.

Designs were drawn up for some of the largest gardens ever seen. Half way through the work, William realised that he couldn't see the river from his new rooms and ordered that the end of the Privy Garden be lowered. Imagine how fed up the workmen must have been!

LOOK OUT FOR...

...the Banqueting House used by William for small parties.

◀ Jean Tijou, a French blacksmith, designed these iron gates. They were painted with **real gold**.

Amazing

One part of the garden had four mazes. They were great places to meet in secret, gossip – and to get lost! One of the mazes still survives. Find out what fun it is to meet in the middle.

▲ Tulips were very fashionable – so William and Mary had lots.

Unpaid bills

The changes to Hampton Court cost millions in today's money. Sadly, William did not live long enough to enjoy his new palace. He left huge debts and Queen Anne, who succeeded him, refused to pay his bills. Many workmen went unpaid.

◀ The Hampton Court Maze.

William died in a fall from his horse that stumbled over a molehill in the park at Hampton Court.

In 1889, Jerome K Jerome wrote **Three Men in a Boat.** In it he described people in the Maze who thought they'd never get out and see their friends and family again!

Right royal rows

During the 1700s, Queen Anne, George I and George II preferred other palaces. Finally, the royal family stopped coming to Hampton Court.

Anne became queen in 1702. Poor Anne had seventeen children but only one son survived – and he died when he was just 11. She grew so fat she could hardly walk – but it didn't stop her hunting in the park.

German George

George I came to throne in 1714. He spent most of his time in Germany. His son, the Prince of Wales (later George II), and his wife Caroline, held wonderful parties at Hampton Court. It caused huge family rows! The quarrels got so bad that George I banned his son from all the royal palaces.

▲ *George II and Queen Caroline*

George II was the last king ▷ *to live at Hampton Court. Look out for his coat of arms on the Trophy Gate as you leave.*

FASTER! FASTER!

◄ George II was very fond of his second son, William, Duke of Cumberland. George had lots of rooms specially built for him. Imagine how Prince Frederick felt about that!

LOOK OUT FOR...

...the Great Vine planted in 1768. Today, it's the oldest vine in the world.

This stone guard props up the fireplace in the Queen's Guard Chamber. ▼

Like father, like son

When the Prince of Wales became George II in 1727, he too fell out with his son, Prince Frederick. They disliked each other so much that Frederick swore that none of his children would be born under the same roof as his parents! When Frederick's wife, Princess Augusta, was about to have a baby at Hampton Court, she was whisked away to St James's Palace in the middle of the night.

Queen Anne followed the hunt in a two-wheeled cart which she drove herself at high speed.

She's got it in for me!

One of Queen Caroline's Ladies of the Bedchamber was Henrietta Howard, George II's girlfriend. The Queen gave her the worst jobs to do.

Home sweet home

From 1760 onwards, Hampton Court became home to poor relations of the royal family, crusty old nobles, famous generals, daring explorers and a professor or two.

Hampton Court was divided into about 60 apartments. These were known as grace-and-favour homes because they were given rent free by the 'grace and favour' (permission) of royalty. Many apartments were very large but often had no bathrooms or heating.

Moans and grumbles

There were lots of complaints from the residents. The seating in the Chapel Royal was a big cause of trouble. People had to sit strictly in order of rank and importance. Some elderly ladies behaved very badly by squabbling about who should sit where.

▲ The residents put on plays, sometimes in the Great Hall.

▼ Residents used an old sedan chair called 'the Push' for getting around the palace.

Oh get out and push yourself!

Residents were only allowed to keep small house-trained dogs. Some kept large retrievers or alsatians, saying that they were allowed because the dogs were well-behaved.

Famous residents

Princesses Bamba, Catherine and Sophia Duleep Singh, the daughters of the Maharaja Duleep Singh, lived at Hampton Court in the early 20th century. They became Suffragettes (women who fought for the same rights to vote as men).

Lady Baden-Powell, founder of the Girl Guides, had an apartment in Henry VIII's Kitchens. Her bath was in one of the fireplaces!

▲ Princesses Bamba and Catherine Duleep Singh.

▲ Children in class at Hampton Court in the 1950s.

School days

Hampton Court had its own school for children of residents and those who worked at the palace. The children were said to be 'clean, quiet and orderly'! The school closed in 1954.

GOOD DAY SIR

MADAM

Lady Gordon was told off for allowing water to pour through the floor damaging pictures in the Queen's Private Apartments below.

A stitch in time

▲ Hampton Court chimneys

▼ Conservators working on the heads of Roman emperors from Cardinal Wolsey's palace. They use the latest technology to stop them falling apart.

Today over half a million people visit Hampton Court every year including lots and lots of school children. Hooray!

All visitors cause wear and tear on the palace – including **you**. A team of specially trained men and women (conservators) work all year round to clean, repair and restore the palace.

Like many old things, parts wear out. Hampton Court has 241 decorative brick chimneys - the largest collection in England. Over time the weather has made them crumble. Now all of them need to be repaired – and **each brick costs £10!**

▲ Tapestries and textiles are cleaned and repaired in studios in the palace.

Every year conservators spend many hours peeling off over 2kg of chewing gum from the State Apartments' floors.

HAVE YOU TRIED UPSTAIRS YET?

Insects called woolly bears like feasting on textiles. The dyes stain their tummies.

Hungry bugs

It's not only visitors that cause damage. Each year conservators trap about 8000 insects that love to eat and make their homes in wooden floors and furniture, silk curtains and woollen textiles.

New discoveries

Historians, conservators and archaeologists are always making new discoveries about Hampton Court. Historians might discover old records, conservators sometimes reveal long lost details and archaeologists find new information by carefully digging the palace up.

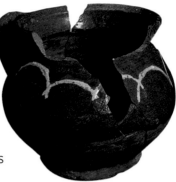

▲ *Archaeologists found this Tudor potty. Who do you think it belonged to?*

◀ *The palace once had its own fire brigade.*

▼ *In 1986 William III's Apartments were badly damaged by fire. It took conservators six years to restore them.*

A grand day out

In 1838 Queen Victoria opened Hampton Court to the public. When the railway opened ten years later, it became a very popular day out for Londoners.

Although not many other palaces were open to the public then, not everyone was pleased. The residents living in the grace-and-favour apartments thought their lives would be **wrecked** by hordes of noisy day-trippers.

▲ In 1912, it cost 10p to get into Hampton Court.

▲ A poster advertising Hampton Court in 1923.

◀ The palace gardens were famous for their flower borders. They still are! In the summer, a military band played to visitors.

Residents thought crowds of people would march through Hampton Court tearing down tapestries, wrecking the furniture and carrying off paintings!

The Hampton Court Palace Ghost.

The Ghost of Catherine Howard, wife of Hen[...]d to be seen at night rush-
ing through the Great Hall. She stops su[...]ging her hands shrieks
despairingly, then returns and disappea[...]the haunted chamber.

◀ *An old postcard of the 'ghost' of Catherine Howard. Can you see the executioner's ghost creeping up behind her?*

LOOK OUT FOR...

...this lion sticking his tongue out in the Horn Room! Can you see Queen Victoria's initials on his shield?

Today, thousands of visitors still come to see where Henry VIII once ruled, to marvel at William and Mary's magnificent State Apartments and to admire the gardens. Once Hampton Court belonged to kings and queens. Today it belongs to **YOU**. So three cheers for Queen Victoria!

Hip, hip, hooray!

LET'S HAVE SOME FUN

The stories of ghosts at Hampton Court were very popular. People expected to see one round every corner!

33

What happened when . . .

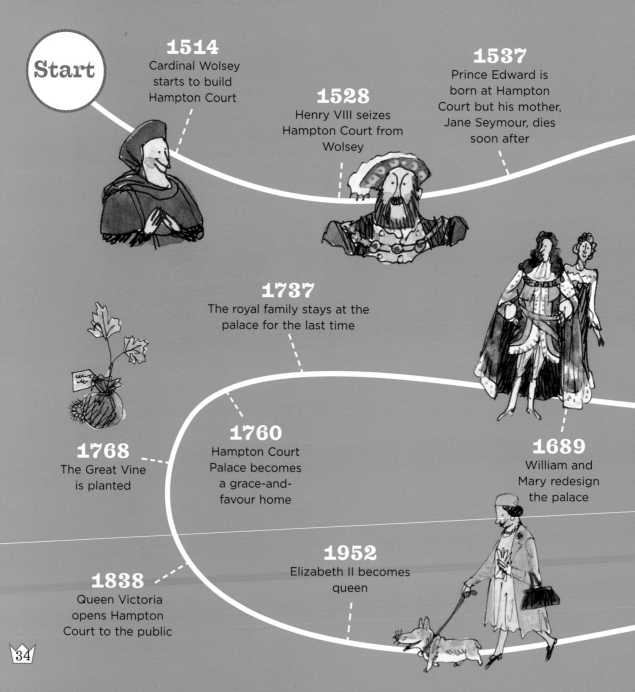

Start

1514
Cardinal Wolsey starts to build Hampton Court

1528
Henry VIII seizes Hampton Court from Wolsey

1537
Prince Edward is born at Hampton Court but his mother, Jane Seymour, dies soon after

1737
The royal family stays at the palace for the last time

1768
The Great Vine is planted

1760
Hampton Court Palace becomes a grace-and-favour home

1689
William and Mary redesign the palace

1838
Queen Victoria opens Hampton Court to the public

1952
Elizabeth II becomes queen